To ....

YOU have **my** HEART

From..

For Mum. You will always have my heart.
— Corinne

To my mother.
— Robin

The Five Mile Press Pty Ltd
1 Centre Road, Scoresby
Victoria 3179 Australia
www.fivemile.com.au

Part of the Bonnier Publishing Group
www.bonnierpublishing.com

First published 2016

Printed in China 5 4 3 2 1

YOU have my HEART

by Corinne Fenton
and Robin Cowcher

The Five Mile Press

On sunshine-inside-of-me days

tears-tumbling-down days

mountain-too-high days

and on the days
I could SCREAM!

On I-can-jump-puddles days

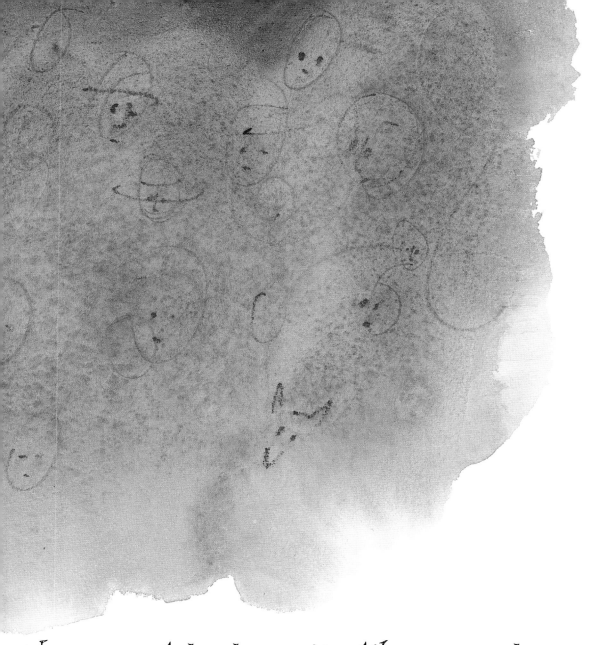

the-world-doesn't-like-me days

and all the days

in–between...

You lift me higher,

make me stronger —

you have my heart.